Funny You Should Say That

Funny You Should Say That

ROY WILLIAMSON

daybreak

First published in 1992 by
Daybreak
Darton, Longman and Todd Ltd
89 Lillie Road, London SW6 1UD

© 1992 Roy Williamson

Illustrations © 1992 Taffy Davies

ISBN 0–232–51982–X

A catalogue record for this book is available
from the British Library

Cover: illustration Taffy Davies; design Jeremy Dixon

Phototypeset by Intype, London
Printed and bound in Great Britain
at the University Press, Cambridge

To
the millions of listeners
who tune in each day
to *Pause for Thought*

Earth's crammed with heaven,
And every common bush afire with God;
But only he who sees it, takes off his shoes.
The rest sit round it and pluck blackberries.

from 'Aurora Leigh'
by Elizabeth Barrett Browning

Contents

Contents

Introduction

THERE IS OFTEN a very thin line between the holy and the hilarious. That should not surprise us. The teaching of Jesus, though profoundly serious, is permeated with stories that bring a smile to the lips. And in my own limited experience the amusing side of life insists on 'peeping through' even on the most solemn occasion. Indeed the words, actions and attitudes of ordinary people rarely fail to bring me joy and, at the same time, open windows into the character of God.

Time and again in the middle of a conversation my mind registers the response – 'Funny you should say that' – and then rushes off along pathways of imagination and inspiration, sometimes reflecting the serious as well as the humorous aspects of life. As I watch and listen to people I find myself wonderfully encouraged and I am affirmed in my conviction that God is alive and abroad in his world. At times his footsteps may appear faint or indistinct, but they are there. Those who have eyes to see them and the curiosity, if not the faith, to follow them, will catch glimpses of his glory and learn to stand in awe at the presence of God in the ordinary.

These twenty-five short chapters are a selection of *Pause for Thoughts* from the *Breakfast Show* on Radio Two. To each has been added a Scripture reading and prayer, which may help the reader towards further reflection and, perhaps, practical action.

The *Pause for Thought* slot lasts only a couple of minutes – though it is followed by a fairly lively chat-back between contributor and DJ. It is amazing just how much can be contained in so short a time but the general principle is to concentrate on one main point. To do this in such a manner as to hold the interest of a largely 'secular' audience and at the same time communicate some important aspect of religious truth is a demanding task. However, since those listening are numbered not in thousands but in millions, it is well worth the effort. Certainly it would take a lifetime of church sermons to reach a fraction of those who listen to *Pause for Thought* on any one morning.

Those who observed and wrote about the life of Jesus remarked that, 'Large crowds listened to him with delight.' He began where people were. He told stories and used metaphors to get his message across. This was the language of God. People could relate to it. It referred to those things which were part of their everyday experience. It reached right into the human heart and touched hidden chords of longing and response.

What follows in this little book is a sincere, though inevitably inadequate, attempt to follow the example and the pattern laid down by Jesus, the master story-teller. Many of those who listened to him simply enjoyed the stories without appreciating the wonder and the challenge of the truths being communicated. They sat around and enjoyed the story for the story's sake. Others, while enjoying the story, glimpsed deeper meaning and eagerly pressed for further light and truth which, when it was given, produced awe and wonder, worship and joy.

Introduction

The ordinary aspects of human life can, with the help of God's creative Spirit, be set ablaze with the life and glory of God. In this sense I believe that heaven can be anticipated every day and I long for people to recognise it and enter into the wonder of it. It is out of such a conviction that these simple words are written. A conviction, borne out by daily experience, that earth is crammed with heaven.

1

Remembering

I'M FASCINATED BY THE different methods people use to make sure they remember things. Some tie a knot in their handkerchief. Schoolchildren scribble words on the back of their hands. A friend of mine writes herself little notes which she then pins up all over the house – and still she forgets. My own particular method is a bit weird. I'm one of those annoying people whose mind works overtime in the wee small hours of the morning. Frequently I remember important things in the middle of the night and, to make sure I don't forget them again, I grab a book from my bedside table and throw it onto the floor. Sometimes when I get out of bed in the morning the floor looks like a minefield. But it seems to work. I can't avoid falling over the books and so I recall the things I wish to remember.

Remembering things is relatively easy. Remembering people, especially their names, is not quite so simple, particularly when they come up to you in the street, or at some function or other, and assume that because you met them for fifteen seconds fifteen years ago you can

remember precisely who they are. People tend to recognise me because my purple shirt is a 'dead give-away'. So they have the advantage over me while I struggle like fury to remember who they are. To forget may be unforgivable.

The classic encounter took place in a local hospital. I had gone in for a little exploratory operation. A local anaesthetic was all that was needed so when I was wheeled into the theatre I wasn't 'zonked out' but fairly relaxed. Indeed with the help of the pre-med I was perhaps a trifle blasé. Suddenly a pair of eyes looked down at me and said, 'You don't recognise me, do you?' It must have been the eyes that spoke because I couldn't see any lips moving! The body was covered with a green gown, the head was covered with a green cap, the face, apart from the eyes, was covered with a green mask. 'You don't recognise me, do you?' Well I ask you. I hadn't a hope! Now I have a little formula which helps me extricate myself in such circumstances but I am keeping it to myself. I mustn't give away my pastoral secrets though I can say that on this rather unique occasion honour was satisfied all round.

But it all helps to emphasise the value people place on being recognised and remembered, if possible by name. I suppose that is why, when God spoke to people in Bible days, he didn't say 'Hey you', but called them by name. Indeed, he was so determined to remember them that he followed the example of the schoolchildren – 'I have written', he said, 'your name on the palms of my hands'. That is a quaint and rather poetic way of saying that God never forgets us. When he opens his hands to do things he always has us in mind.

Now, of course, God doesn't have hands. Nor does he have elasticated arms to stretch down from heaven. But he does have your hands and mine. They are the practical means by which he shows his care for people and reveals that they are remembered and not forgotten. Who can doubt, for instance, that in those slums of Calcutta today, the hands on the end of the arms of Mother Teresa are the hands of God. Indeed, in the hospitals and hospices throughout our own country this very day, wherever disease is healed, pain is eased or fear is removed there the hands of God are at work – and people know they are not forgotten.

SCRIPTURES TO READ

And now, thus says Yahweh,
he who created you, Jacob,
  who formed you, Israel:
Do not be afraid, for I have redeemed you;
I have called you by your name, you are mine.
Should you pass through the waters,
  I shall be with you;
or through rivers,
  they will not swallow you up.
Should you walk through fire, you will not suffer,
and the flame will not burn you.
For I am Yahweh, your God,
the Holy One of Israel, your Saviour.

(Isaiah 43:1–3)

Can a woman forget her baby at the breast,
feel no pity for the child she has borne?
Even if these were to forget,
I shall not forget you.
Look, I have engraved you on the palms of my
  hands . . .

(Isaiah 49:15–16)

A PRAYER TO USE

Lord, help us this day to use our hands, our love and
our lives to remind those in any kind of need that they
are not forgotten.

2

Appearances can be Deceptive

THOSE WHO HAVE teenage sons and daughters will understand me when I say that tidiness is not always very high on their list of priorities. Indeed it is considered by some teenagers to be positively old-fashioned. Clothes must be well-worn, jeans must be torn at the knee and bedrooms must appear to have been hit by a cyclone. As for the family sitting-room, with the help of teenagers it can look like the aftermath of World War Three – bodies, coffee cups, magazines, cassettes and, just occasionally, homework lying in abundant confusion.

And that's only the good news! The bad news is that it doesn't get any better even when they leave home; for when they return they bring chaos with them. The same mix as before only this time, from their university or college bedsits, they produce two or three weeks' supply of dirty washing. It's contained in a bag or suitcase which is nonchalantly dropped by the front door on their arrival and picked up with equal nonchalance on their departure. With the clear assumption, of course, that the good fairy or, if you happen to be Irish, the 'Little People' have washed and ironed it all in the meantime.

Now the truth of the matter is that, despite their protests, parents wouldn't really have it any other way. It's nice to be needed. Besides, home is a place where our teenagers can be themselves without pretence. But it does have its problems. You see, I have two matching suitcases. The one I keep for carrying my episcopal robes to church services. The other I gave to my son for transporting his clothes to and from college. Like him I place my case by the front door, ready for loading into the car. Well, it's the natural thing to do, isn't it? Yes, but things aren't always what they appear to be. And last week I picked up the wrong case, discovering just in time that a mud-covered rugby shirt and a set of 'grubby undies' were not appropriate garments for a bishop to wear in a church procession. But I think my son might have been more embarrassed than me if he had turned up at college wearing a cope and mitre!

When I had recovered from the shock and had a good laugh about it I resolved to be a little more careful in future. It's one thing getting a couple of suitcases mixed up but it becomes more serious where the lives of people are concerned and when we judge them by appearances – and get it wrong.

Like the story in the Bible about the choice of David to be king of Israel. The powers that be had put him at the bottom of their short-list. He didn't appear to be the right person at all. Too young and too inexperienced they reckoned. But God turned their short-list upside-down. He didn't judge according to appearances but according to the heart – and David was made king. And God got it right – as poor Goliath later discovered to his cost.

So many of the people with whom Jesus mixed while on earth were considered by the rulers, even the religious rulers, to be either a nuisance or an inconvenience. Jesus saw beyond the superficial classifications of men and women, and in the lives of ordinary people he discovered pure gold. Before we pass judgement, if we must pass judgement, on other people we need to get to know them better.

SCRIPTURES TO READ

'Take no notice of his appearance or his height . . . God does not see as human beings see; they look at appearances but Yahweh looks at the heart.'

(1 Samuel 16:7)

'Do not judge, and you will not be judged; because the judgements you give are the judgements you will get, and the standard you use will be the standard used for you. Why do you observe the splinter in your brother's eye and never notice the great log in your own? And how dare you say to your brother, "Let me take that splinter out of your eye," when look, there is a great log in your own? Hypocrite! Take the log out of your own eye first, and then you will see clearly enough to take the splinter out of your brother's eye.'

(Matthew 7:1–5)

A PRAYER TO USE

Please keep us, O God, from premature and harsh judgements and give us a generous spirit towards other people.

3

Sorrow turned to Joy

EMBARRASSING MOMENTS are common to us all. Those dreadful experiences in life when we wish the ground would open and swallow us up. I have had my share of such moments and I still go hot and cold every time I think of them. Two weeks ago I was witness to somebody else's embarrassing moment and my heart went out to them.

It was at a wedding reception. The eighty guests were thoroughly enjoying the wedding feast and had reached the sweet course. To gasps of delight and expectancy the waitress wheeled in the sweet trolley piled high with a great variety of goodies. It was her big moment and she made the most of it as she repeated constantly the selection that was on offer. She completed her service to the first table and turned from the ten very satisfied customers to the next table. That's when her troubles began. The trolley was heavy and needed a good strong pull. She obliged, but the wheels stuck, the trolley tipped, then tumbled and every single item on it cascaded onto the carpet. Black Forest gateaux mingled disgustingly with sherry trifles, profiteroles wallowed in the sludge of crème caramel, orange sorbet was introduced rather unceremoniously to chocolate mousse and the fruit salad – well, that was everywhere!

I have never seen such a mess or witnessed such embarrassment. Everyone was embarrassed and none more so that the poor waitress. My own embarrassment was relieved by a flight of fancy as I imagined the reception being held in Fawlty Towers with Basil striding about in total panic pretending he was in complete control of the situation. It was Sybil's fault, of course, but it was Manuel he sent for and it was Manuel who managed to make a chaotic situation even worse and who was now being cuffed about the ears for his efforts!

Thankfully I came back to reality for the facts were even more remarkable than the fantasy.

Three waitresses had appeared with the sound of the crashing trolley. Within seconds the mess was cleared. With enormous aplomb and to a great and spontaneous round of applause the waitress entered the dining room wheeling another sweet trolley with an even greater selection of goodies on it. It was a masterly entrance and the applause was well-deserved, though this expression of pleasure on the part of the guests had as much to do with the relief of their embarrassment as with hers. They were genuinely delighted that tragedy had been so quickly turned to triumph.

Now I have no doubt that the waitress would have preferred the incident never to have taken place. She, like me, will never forget it, which is why I mention it today for it keeps reminding me of one of the deeper truths of life as well as of Christianity. When adversity or misfortune comes, God doesn't usually 'zap' in, wave a magic wand and remove the difficult circumstances.

More often than not it is by working through the diffi-
culties that they are resolved. The raw material of life
becomes the raw material for both tragedy and triumph.
I think this is what our Lord meant when he said to his
disciples who were so sorrowful at the prospect of being
left alone, 'Your sorrow will be turned into joy'.

SCRIPTURES TO READ

'In all truth I tell you, you will be weeping and wailing
while the world will rejoice; you will be sorrowful, but
your sorrow will turn to joy. A woman in childbirth
suffers, because her time has come; but when she has
given birth to the child she forgets the suffering in her
joy that a human being has been born into the world.
So it is with you: you are sad now, but I shall see you
again, and your hearts will be full of joy, and that joy
no one shall take from you.'

(John 16:20–2)

In the evening of that same day, the first day of the
week, the doors were closed in the room where the
disciples were, for fear of the Jews. Jesus came and
stood among them. He said to them, 'Peace be with
you', and, after saying this, he showed them his hands
and his side. The disciples were filled with joy at
seeing the Lord.

(John 20:19, 20)

A PRAYER TO USE

Lord, as you transformed the sorrow of the crucifixion
into the joy of the Resurrection, so may you bring peace

into the lives of all who are distressed and turn their sorrow into joy.

4

Power

MY THREE YOUNG GRANDSONS are staying with me at present and, as you can imagine, there isn't a dull moment. But I am helping to keep them amused by telling them some of my stories – like the one about the fire-engine at the local airport.

They thought I was joking at first but I really did have a hair-raising ride on the airport fire-engine. You see, I regularly visit local industry and a few weeks ago I went to the local airport to learn at first hand of the incredible amount of organisation and efficiency that is required for the safety and comfort of passengers. It was all very impressive but the highlight of the visit was undoubtedly the ride on the fire-engine. When the director offered me the opportunity, there was no hesitation. All my boyhood enthusiasm reasserted itself and I was soon racing across the tarmac in a massive machine which, in about twenty seconds, was able to reach a speed of eighty miles an hour.

It was exhilarating. But the most exciting part was still to come for as we reached the practice area the senior officer invited me onto the roof of the vehicle to take control of the water-cannon. He then switched on the water supply and I thundered down the runway at eighty miles an hour spreading powerful jets of water in all directions – and thinking wicked thoughts like, 'Could I work myself out of a job by baptising the whole of my diocese in one fell swoop?' But the overriding feeling was one of immense power – which I had under my control.

That's a feeling, of course, that some people and nations have all the time. Power is the name of the game and whether it is economic, industrial or military power, or simply the power of personality, it is considered to be the key to success. The desire for power is to be seen in every walk of life and the Church is no exception. Power only becomes a problem when we haven't got any!

But it is the abuse of power that causes trouble. Employers can abuse it in relation to their employees. Parents can abuse it with regard to their children and, as we all know, the peace of the world is frequently threatened by the misuse of power in some nations. Yet power can be a tremendous force for good. The power of science and technology, for instance, has brought healing, health and happiness to millions of people – and the power of the airport fire-engine has prevented tragedy, limited disaster and saved life.

It is not without significance that Jesus, whose power created the universe, chose to lead people by example rather than drive them by force. He chose to serve them rather than control them. Now that's a proper use of power.

Those of us who possess and have opportunities to exercise power need to remember that, wisely used, power doesn't try to control, manipulate or hammer people into submission. On the contrary – it sets them free!

SCRIPTURES TO READ

> Thus says the High and Exalted One
> who lives eternally
> and whose name is holy,
> 'I live in the holy heights
> but I am with the contrite and humble,
> to revive the spirit of the humble,
> to revive the heart of the contrite.'
>
> (Isaiah 57:15)

An argument also began between them [his disciples] about who should be reckoned the greatest; but he said to them, 'Among the gentiles it is the kings who lord it over them, and those who have authority over them are given the title Benefactor. With you this must not happen. No; the greatest among you must behave as if he were the youngest, the leader as if he were the one who serves. For who is the greater: the one at table or the one who serves? The one at table, surely? Yet here am I among you as one who serves!'

(Luke 22:24–7)

A PRAYER TO USE

Lord, may we use the power we possess to set people free rather than increase their dependence. And on those occasions when we ourselves feel powerless help us not to despair but to learn how to rest in your strength.

5

Carry Each Other's Burdens

IT MAY SEEM A STRANGE THING for a bishop to say but one of the drawbacks of my job is that I have to go to church rather a lot. The old quip that the clergy on six days of the week are invisible and on the seventh incomprehensible is not entirely accurate as far as I am concerned. All too often I am visible in church – sometimes seven days a week. It can be a trial at times – as well as being a little sore on the knees!

However, there are occasions when it becomes a bit special. Time when, to use a modern expression, I actually touch base. Times when I encounter reality. Something happens which leaves me in no doubt whatsoever that I have been in the presence of God and he has communicated with me. Like a few nights ago when I was at a service in London. Now that was a service to remember!

No, it wasn't in St Paul's or Westminster Abbey or one of the other famous London churches but in a little-known church south of the river. The parish, which is densely populated by Afro-Caribbeans, was welcoming

15

a new vicar. The service was lively and colourful. There was a festival atmosphere – with lots of people, lots of music and some wonderful singing. Children were everywhere and not least in the Bishop's Procession as it moved into church. As they marched in procession they carried banners and balloons and I couldn't keep my feet from tapping as the steel band hammered out its syncopated rhythm of 'Oh when the saints go marching in'!

It was marvellous and I was having a wonderful time when I became aware that something wasn't quite right. I spotted that the Processional Cross was not being held high enough nor carried straight enough. Fussy individual that I am, it annoyed me at first. Why wasn't it being carried properly, I thought to myself, as it drew near to where I was sitting? And then, suddenly, I saw that not only was it being carried properly but it was also being carried beautifully and bravely in the hands of a severely disabled and extremely attractive young West Indian woman. She held the cross proudly and firmly and as high and straight as she could – from the wheelchair in which she sat and in which she was being pushed by a friend.

That was the most moving moment I have experienced in church for a very long time. I felt rebuked for my earlier critical thoughts and I felt uplifted by the modern-day parable that I was witnessing. She could never have walked into church carrying that cross. She was one saint who simply couldn't 'go marching in'. But with the help of a friend, she made it – and enriched my life and the lives of hundreds of others that night. She personified a great truth – that God is the God of paradox. He expresses his power in humility. He chooses the weak to challenge the strong. He uses those who appear

16

to have nothing to rebuke those who believe they have everything.

There are lots of disabled – or, perhaps, more accurately, differently abled – people in this world of ours. They have a wonderful contribution to make to so many areas of life. All they need is a little help from those of us who are less disabled. The Bible writer got to the heart of the matter when he advised – if you want to obey the law of the love of Christ you must learn to carry each other's burdens.

SCRIPTURES TO READ

God's folly is wiser than human wisdom, and God's weakness is stronger than human strength. Consider . . . how you were called; not many of you are wise by human standards, not many influential, not many from noble families. No, God chose those who by human standards are fools to shame the wise; he chose those who by human standards are weak to shame the strong; those who by human standards are common and contemptible – indeed those who count for nothing – to reduce to nothing all those that do count for something, so that no human being might feel boastful before God.

(1 Corinthians 1:25–8)

Carry each other's burdens; that is how to keep the law of Christ.

(Galatians 6:2)

A PRAYER TO USE

Thank you, God, for the strength you give to us even in times of weakness and for the courage of those who triumph over disabilities to serve others. Give grace and patience to the disabled and love and understanding to those who care for them, and may we never forget that none of us is perfect and wholeness is only to be found in you.

6

It's the Little Things that Matter

'IT's NOT THE BIG THINGS that worry me. It's the little things that get me down.' Those words were spoken recently by a friend of mine when I tried to comfort her at a time of great trouble in her life. Bishops are supposed to be good at words of sympathy, though there are times when even we can put both feet in it. However, on this particular occasion I thought I had got it right, only to be met with the surprising response, 'Oh, it's not the big things that worry me. It's the little things that get me down.' As though to illustrate the point she was making my friend's main concern, it seemed, in the midst of all her trouble, was who would look after the budgie while she was away.

On reflection what she said contained an enormous amount of practical wisdom. When life's major crises come upon us, in whatever form, our family and friends rally round to help. We receive an immense amount of sympathy, understanding and support and, in some strange way, we can draw upon reserves of strength to help us through the sticky patch.

19

But so often it is the silly, niggling little things that get on our nerves, disturb the harmony of the household and leave us frustrated and annoyed. The washing machine goes wrong and the water floods all over the kitchen floor just five minutes before we are due to go on holiday. The car gets stuck in a traffic jam and throws our whole schedule out for the rest of the day. Or, perhaps, like another friend of mine recently, whose dress suit had been returned from the cleaners with the wrong pair of trousers. He only discovered the mistake five minutes before he went out to attend an important civic function. No big deal, you might say, until you realised that my friend was built like Ronnie Corbett and the trousers obviously belonged to Cyril Smith. In

his particular case it was not so much the little things as the large things that got him down!

So I have to admit that my troubled friend's philosophy of life is not so far off the mark. Indeed it helps me to understand some of the more remarkable aspects of the life of Jesus. Here he was, engaged apparently in the most tremendous task of winning the world for God, yet he spent his time talking and listening to the socially insignificant. He shows concern for a couple who have to borrow bread from a neighbour because friends have arrived unexpectedly. He expresses a similar concern for a woman who is upset by the loss of a sentimental coin and for a farmer who is disturbed because one of his sheep is missing. Perhaps most remarkable of all, his motivation for feeding the multitude was not just the fact that they were hungry. He was genuinely concerned as to how the crowds would get home – since they had followed him all day and were liable to faint with hunger. To my shame, I don't think I have ever been concerned about such a thing. My anxiety has been how to get people *to* church without worrying how they might get home!

I think there is something really important here. So often we feel helpless in the face of other people's tragedies, whether they be national, like the Hillsborough Disaster, or personal, like the death of a husband, wife, child or close friend. There seems so little we can do to help. But when we remember that life must go on and daily problems must be faced there dawns the realisation that our caring must also continue and be expressed in ordinary, practical and everyday matters. It is at that level that our help can be so useful and so necessary, for it is not always the big things that worry people. It's the little things that get them down.

SCRIPTURES TO READ

Jesus said to them, 'Suppose one of you has a friend and goes to him in the middle of the night to say, "My friend, lend me three loaves, because a friend of mine on his travels has just arrived at my house and I have nothing to offer him;" and the man answers from inside the house, "Do not bother me. The door is bolted now, and my children are with me in bed; I cannot get up to give it to you." I tell you, if the man does not get up and give it to him for friendship's sake, persistence will make him get up and give his friend all he wants.'

(Luke 11:5–8)

But Jesus called his disciples to him and said, 'I feel sorry for all these people; they have been with me for three days now and have nothing to eat. I do not want to send them off hungry, or they might collapse on the way.' The disciples said to him, 'Where in a deserted place could we get sufficient bread for such a large crowd to have enough to eat?' Jesus said to them, 'How many loaves have you?' They said, 'Seven, and a few small fish.' Then he instructed the crowd to sit down on the ground, and he took the seven loaves and the fish, and after giving thanks he broke them and began handing them to the disciples, who gave them to the crowds. They all ate as much as they wanted, and they collected what was left of the scraps, seven baskets full. Now four thousand men had eaten, to say nothing of women and children. And when he had sent the crowds away he got into the boat and went to the territory of Magadan.

(Matthew 15:32–9)

A PRAYER TO USE

We thank you, our Father, that you are interested in the detail of ordinary life. May we show a similar concern towards other people. Make us sensitive to their needs and willing to offer practical help in times of trouble.

7

Stewardship

Every bishop, as well as having the care of his own diocese, must also carry some central responsibility in the Church. My current responsibility concerns stewardship and I spend a lot of my time trying to widen people's vision as to what the term really means.

Many people have a slightly jaundiced view of the term and see it as a posh name for separating people from their money in order to bump up the church collections. That is actually a travesty of the truth. To see stewardship simply as an 'in' word for religious people is to ignore the fact that it addresses one of the major issues of our time in which every single one of us is involved. Basically it refers to our responsible care and use of everything that is given to us in this world.

The lessons we learn best in life are nearly always those we are forced to learn the hard way. This particular lesson I learnt as a result of a moment of great embarrassment several years ago when I was driving through Margaret Thatcher's home town of Grantham. At the time I was caught in a long line of cars at some

24

traffic lights. Having both hands free for a moment I took the opportunity to pop a piece of chocolate into my mouth and bung the wrapping paper out of the window. I was just about to close the window when a policeman appeared – holding my wrapping paper in his hand. 'Sir,' he said, 'we are trying to keep our town as clean as possible. Please take your rubbish with you when you leave.' If only the ground could have opened and swallowed me up!

But, since divine intervention of that kind seemed out of the question, I muttered an embarrassed apology, took the wrapping paper, let in the clutch and, at a discreet speed, of course, left the scene of the crime! As I drove away I was full of anger. To be honest, I was angry at being caught and embarrassed. But, on reflection, I ended up being full of admiration for the courtesy and concern of the unknown constable who had taught me a lesson I have never forgotten – which is why it so readily comes to mind.

We are all responsible for the care of our environment. If we misuse or exploit it through indifference or self-interest our grandchildren will be the ones to suffer – and they won't thank us for it.

Now we all have our own horror stories to tell about pollution, acid rain, the ozone layer, the greenhouse effect, the tons of litter removed daily from our streets – and we can reach the stage when we become paralysed by the sheer size of the problem. So we 'back off' and leave it to other people to do something about it. Of course, it isn't always easy to get the balance of concern right. The issues are not nearly as clear-cut as some would have us believe, but all of us have some small corner in which we can demonstrate our care for the environment. There are practical things that we each can do, like the use of unleaded petrol and ozone-friendly aerosols. We might even keep our chocolate wrappings in the car rather than throw them out the window.

World leaders and national politicians have been forced to put global stewardship towards the top of their agenda but they are only catching up on what our Creator did a long time ago. God saw all that he had made – *and it was very good*. We live in a beautiful world. It makes sense to look after it for it is both God's world *and our home*.

SCRIPTURES TO READ

God blessed them, saying to them, 'Be fruitful, multiply, fill the earth and subdue it. Be masters of the fish of the sea, the birds of heaven and all the living creatures that move on earth.' God also said, 'Look, to you I give all the seed-bearing plants everywhere on the surface of the earth, and all the trees with seed-bearing fruit; this will be your food. And to all the wild animals, all the birds of heaven and all the living creatures that creep along the ground, I give all the foliage of the plants as their food.' And so it was. God saw all that he had made, and indeed it was very good.

(Genesis 1:28–31)

A PRAYER TO USE

God, the Creator of all, you have given us the privilege and responsibility of being stewards of your beautiful world. May we so enjoy our privilege and discharge our responsibility that our grandchildren may rejoice and

give thanks for the wonders of creation and the beauty
of their environment.

8

Cordless Telephones

L IKE MOST OTHER PEOPLE I get frustrated when
trains don't run on time. Nevertheless, I like travelling by train and thoroughly enjoy my trips from the
North to King's Cross on the Intercity 125 – especially
now that I've discovered that en route entertainment is
a distinct possibility.

One of the pleasures of travelling by train has been
to get away from the telephone. Three hours of freedom
from its incessant demands has provided a glorious
opportunity for a good read or a sound sleep. Yesterday,
being Monday, reading was on the menu. I had had
enough religion the day before so it was time for a dose
of escapism in the form of a novel by Dick Francis. But
it was not to be.

The train had reached Peterborough and I had
reached page thirty-five when I heard the sound of not
one telephone but two. Immediately I felt the urge to
answer them but, of course, there was no need. Each of
the two young men opposite me plunged a hand into
a pocket and produced a cordless telephone. A quick

extension of aerials and conversation began. And so it continued throughout the remainder of the journey to King's Cross. Every few minutes the telephone rang and if my two travelling companions were not receiving calls they were making them – constantly consulting their 'fil-o-fax' and ringing their secretaries for 'up-dates' on the current situation.

I was fascinated. I kept my eyes on the Dick Francis but I wasn't reading a word. I couldn't concentrate. There was more drama taking place on the seat opposite me than there was in the novel in my hand. As a young boy I remember being given a 'thick ear' for opening the doors of telephone boxes and listening to other people's conversations. Now I was being given a ringside seat – and my ears felt like satellite dishes!

It was all very entertaining and a little embarrassing for I was forced to hear several things that were none of my business. I'm not complaining, mind you, curious beggar that I am. But I couldn't help feeling sorry for the poor secretary being constantly bothered by her ubiquitous boss just when she had relaxed in the knowl-edge that he was safely out of harm's way on a train from Bradford to London.

I am sure it was necessary for all those 'phone calls to be made – even though the train was travelling to its destination at very high speed. Perhaps to anticipate their arrival by a few minutes was crucial for the business success of my two fellow-travellers (though I do remem-ber that one of the final calls was an exhortation to put the kettle on!). It was symbolic, I think, of the pace of modern life and the increasingly urgent need to antici-pate tomorrow. We have even begun to anticipate the next millennium and are constantly being exhorted to prepare for the year two thousand. But what about today? Some of us have become so intent upon tomorrow that we tend to forget about today.

Of course it makes sense to plan in advance. We would be foolish if we didn't. Jesus' words, 'Take no thought for tomorrow', if taken out of context and pushed to their illogical conclusion, would put most insurance companies out of business and drive most normal people up the wall. But their true meaning makes a great deal of sense. We should not become so bogged down with tomorrow's burdens that we fail to appreciate today's blessings.

SCRIPTURES TO READ

'That is why I am telling you not to worry about your life and what you are to eat, nor about your body and what you are to wear. Surely life is more than food, and the body more than clothing! Look at the birds in the sky. They do not sow or reap or gather into barns; yet your heavenly Father feeds them. Are you not worth much more than they are? Can any of you, however much you worry, add one single cubit to your span of life? And why worry about clothing? Think of the flowers growing in the field; they never have to work or spin; yet I assure you that not even Solomon in all his royal robes was clothed like one of these. Now if that is how God clothes the wild flowers growing in the field which are there today and thrown into the furnace tomorrow, will he not much more look after you, you who have so little faith? So do not worry; do not say, "What are we to eat? What are we to drink? What are we to wear?" It is the gentiles who set their hearts on all these things. Your heavenly Father knows you need them all. Set your hearts on his kingdom first, and on God's saving justice, and all these other things will be given you as well. So do not worry about tomorrow: tomorrow will take care of itself. Each day has enough trouble of its own.'

(Matthew 6:25–34)

A PRAYER TO USE

Lord, help us to get our priorities right. Preserve us from being so obsessively concerned with future prosperity that we fail to be grateful for present privileges.

9

Making Mistakes

A COUPLE OF WEEKS AGO I was travelling by train
from Plymouth to York. The journey seemed end-
less for the train appeared to stop at every station. And
at every station the same ritual was performed, not by
the railway staff but by some of the passengers boarding
the train. I had made the mistake of sitting near the
door of the carriage so I got the same ritual question
addressed to me again and again throughout the journey.
'Is this the train for York?'

Mind you, it said so very clearly on every carriage
door and the platform announcements, contrary to popu-
lar opinion, were as clear as crystal – 'The train now
approaching platform one is the 2.50 for York'. Despite
this, the same question was put to me with monotonous
regularity. 'Is this the train for York?' By the time we
had reached Gloucester I was answering the question
before it was asked – and that got me some funny looks
I can tell you!

It wasn't that people couldn't read. It wasn't that
they doubted their own intelligence. They just wanted

to double-check their decision to get on that particular train. They wanted to be sure. Once the train had started they couldn't do much about it – and Penzance is a long way from Plymouth if you really wanted to go to York. They were afraid of making a mistake.

That is a fear which is common to all of us. None of us likes to make mistakes. But, at the human level, mistakes are inevitable. Sometimes they're trivial and sometimes they're disastrous. On occasions they're embarrassing, like the day when I forgot to include the vows in a wedding service. Frequently they are hilarious, like the day when I sat in a church service and listened to the preacher solemnly assure his flock that he undoubtedly believed that Jonah swallowed the whale! At the end of the day human error is one of the facts of life.

I suppose of all the characters I meet in the course of my life and work the ones that sadden me most are those who are so afraid of making a mistake that they become paralysed with indecision. When that happens not only do they suffer agonies of doubt themselves but other people are often driven up the wall with frustration.

Jesus told a challenging little story about three men, two of whom were prepared to make mistakes and the third who wasn't. The first had five talents and he went out into the free-market economy and, taking all the risks of human error, he doubled his investment. The second man had a similar attitude and he turned his two talents into four. The third person, now he was definitely a 'belt and braces' character. No risks for him. The one talent which he had he took, wrapped it up securely, and buried it. He was so scared of making a mistake that he actually made nothing. Others had something to show for the talents they had been given.

33

But he, apart from showing his skill with a shovel, revealed a caution that was paralysing. To give him credit, he didn't make the silly mistake of losing his talent. Instead he made the fatal mistake of not using it and in the end lost it anyway. It's to be hoped that he learned from his mistake, although we can't take that for granted. That goes for us as well, for mistakes can be profitable – if we learn something from them.

SCRIPTURES TO READ

'It is like a man about to go abroad who summoned his servants and entrusted his property to them. To one he gave five talents, to another two, to a third one, each in proportion to his ability. Then he set out on his journey. The man who had received the five talents promptly went and traded with them and made five more. The man who had received two made two more in the same way. But the man who had received one went off and dug a hole in the ground and hid his master's money. Now a long time afterwards, the master of those servants came back and went through his accounts with them. The man who had received the five talents came forward bringing five more. "Sir," he said, "you entrusted me with five talents; here are five more that I have made." His master said to him, "Well done, good and trustworthy servant; you have shown you are trustworthy in small things; I will trust you with greater; come and join in your master's happiness." Next the man with the two talents came forward. "Sir," he said, "you entrusted me with two talents; here are two more that I have made." ... "Well done ... come and join in your master's happiness." Last came forward the man who

34

had the single talent. "Sir," said he, "I had heard that you were a hard man . . . so I was afraid, and I went off and hid your talent in the ground. Here it is; it was yours, you have it back." But his master answered him, "You wicked and lazy servant! . . . you should have deposited my money with the bankers, and on my return I would have got my money back with interest. So now take the talent from him and give it to the man who has the ten talents. For to everyone who has will be given more, and he will have more than enough; but anyone who has not, will be deprived even of what he has." '

(Matthew 25:14–28)

A PRAYER TO USE

Lord, you have placed your trust in us by giving us talents to use according to our ability. Keep us from selfishly withholding them and help us to use them wisely and well for the benefit of all.

10

Party Time

Recently I threw a huge party, invited over 600 guests – and they all turned up! No, it wasn't a formal occasion for adults, with dainty cucumber sandwiches and china tea on the bishop's lawn. It was for 600 lively and excited schoolchildren and their teachers at one of Yorkshire's beauty spots in Wharfedale.

We all have times in life when we feel that at last we are in touch with reality. Something happens; we meet someone or we achieve something and suddenly there is a deep conviction that we are 'in the right place doing the right thing at the right time!' Well, my children's party was one of those rare occasions.

I had just completed a tour of all our sixty-three church schools. It had taken me eighteen months to get round them all. Children and teachers had welcomed me, given me school dinners – and supplied me with stories on which I can dine out for years to come.

After my visit they wrote some hilarious things in their work-books. Here are a few samples: 'Our Bishop is Irish but he can speak English,' and again, 'I thought that bishops were very old and very grey and not very funny.' And here's one that will get me into trouble, 'I thought the Bishop would be like our vicar, but he wasn't, he was nice.' And how about this for a personal job reference? – 'If that Bishop is ever out of work he could get a job as a stand-up comic'!

They drew pictures of me in all my regalia and sent them to me with love. It isn't always flattering to see yourself as others, especially children, see you and some of their drawings of me wearing my cope and mitre had me looking like a ballistic missile. And they wrote me marvellous letters. When I was talking to them in their schools I had dressed up in my coloured vestments, referring to them as my 'party clothes' and my mitre as my 'party hat'. So I kept getting invitations to their birthday parties, but always with the request, 'Come, but please bring your party hat'.

Actually I had been talking to them simply about the love of God and I was delighted that it had come across to the children in such happy terms. Perhaps that's why they all came to the party and why, like me, they all had such a whale of a time. They sang and they worshipped, they pulled crackers and wore party hats, they picnicked and they released 600 balloons, they gave a wonderful performance of Andrew Lloyd Webber's *Joseph and the Amazing Technicolor Dreamcoat* – and they did it all within the context of the love of God! It was an enormous privilege to be present. Here was reality, the very essence of what I am about, a foretaste of the kingdom of God.

Oh, why do we adults turn our religion into such a boring and oft-times miserable affair? We make such hard work of it. Can we not learn from our children? They are not concerned with the niceties of our liturgy, the nuances of our doctrine, nor the stupidity of our divisions. But they can recognise reality and respond to it with spontaneity, enthusiasm and joy. They get to the heart of the matter and sum up the gospel in simple yet sublime terms – *God has laid on a party and we are invited*!

SCRIPTURES TO READ

Jesus said, 'There was a man who gave a great banquet, and he invited a large number of people. When the time for the banquet came, he sent his servant to say to those who had been invited, "Come along: everything is ready now." But all alike started to make excuses. The first said, "I have bought a piece of land and must go and see it. Please accept my apologies." Another said, "I have bought five yoke of oxen and am on my way to try them out. Please accept my apologies." . . . Yet another said, "I have just got married and so am unable to come."

'The servant returned and reported this to his master. Then the householder, in a rage, said to his servant, "Go out quickly into the streets and alleys of the town and bring in here the poor, the crippled, the blind and the lame." "Sir," said the servant, "your orders have been carried out and there is still room." Then the master said to his servant, "Go to the open roads and the hedgerows and press people to come in, to make sure my house is full; because, I tell you, not one of those who were invited shall have a taste of my banquet." '

(Luke 14:16–24)

At this time the disciples came to Jesus and said, 'Who is the greatest in the kingdom of Heaven?' So he called a little child to him whom he set among them. Then he said, 'In truth I tell you, unless you change and become like little children you will never enter the kingdom of Heaven. And so, the one who makes himself as little as this little child is the greatest in the kingdom of Heaven. Anyone who welcomes one little child like this in my name welcomes me.'

(Matthew 18:1–5)

A PRAYER TO USE

God, our Father, forgive us when we take your love for granted or refuse its demands upon our lives. Fill us with a childlike joy at the wonder of it and with an infectious enthusiasm to share it with others.

11

Nothing that is not Holy

Not long ago I was on holiday in Upper Wharfedale, one of the most beautiful of the North Yorkshire Dales, and, at the same time, I unexpectedly fulfilled an unusual ambition.

At the time of year I was there one of the features of rural life is the Country Show. So my wife and I had a rest from hill-walking and went to the local Kilnsey Show. We were not alone – for it seemed that the whole farming community for miles around had turned up. The interest and activity were intense. There was fell-racing and show-jumping; tents displaying all the crafts and skills of the rural community; and knowledgeable farmers leaning over cattle pens and nodding wisely, as experts judged their Suffolk, Blue-faced Leicester and Swaledale sheep. The sights, sounds and smells of country life were everywhere. It was like a clip from *All Creatures Great and Small*, and I fully expected to bump into James Herriot or Mr Farnon at any moment.

The high spot of the show was the Grand Parade when all the prize-winning cattle and the superbly groomed shire horses entered the show-ring. It was a wonderful sight. But for me, the show-stopper was not a bull or a cow, a sheep or a horse, but a stage coach, yes, a stage coach! It had begun life a hundred years ago on the regular run from London to York. Beautifully restored, it had been brought out of retirement and now, drawn by four magnificent horses and with outriders wearing traditional costumes and blowing traditional horns, it thundered round the parade ring, enthralling the thousands of people watching. We were all back in the 1890s on the road from London to York.

But then came the real surprise. I had gone to the show hoping to be lost in the crowd, totally incognito, clerical garb replaced by country tweeds – not a dog-collar in sight. But it was not to be. Suddenly over the public address system came the announcement, 'And now by special invitation the Bishop of Bradford and Mrs Williamson will ride in the stage coach.' My cover was blown! But it was an offer I couldn't refuse – indeed it fulfilled a life-long ambition. And so, with coach-horns blaring, we were paraded before the whole farming community of Upper Wharfedale, about fifteen thousand of them. The only person missing was Dick Turpin. But I tell you what, we enjoyed every minute of it. It was the crowning experience of a memorable day.

Perhaps at this point some of my readers will be wondering when I'm going to slip in the so-called 'religious bit'. The answer is, 'I'm not'. Because the lesson to be learned from rural life is that there is no sharp distinction between the sacred and the secular. After all, the cows need milking on Sunday as on Monday to Saturday. At that marvellous Country Show a farming community met to celebrate the totality of its life. A life derived from God and resourced by God. No part of it is outside his

interest and concern. To put it another way. There is nothing that is not holy.

SCRIPTURES TO READ

God saw all he had made, and indeed it was very good.

(Genesis 1:31)

Finally, brothers, let your minds be filled with everything that is true, everything that is honourable, everything that is upright and pure, everything that

42

we love and admire – with whatever is good and
praiseworthy.

(Philippians 4:8)

Alleluia!

Praise God in his holy place,
praise him in the heavenly vault of his power,
praise him for his mighty deeds,
praise him for all his greatness.

Praise him with fanfare of trumpet,
praise him with harp and lyre,
praise him with tambourines and dancing,
praise him with strings and pipes,
praise him with the clamour of cymbals,
Let everything that breathes praise Yahweh.

Alleluia!

(Psalm 150)

A PRAYER TO USE

O God, the Creator of all, nothing is outside your knowl-
edge and nothing is excluded from your concern. Help
us not to divide our lives into watertight compartments
but to experience and express a unity and wholeness in
all we say and do and are.

12

Remember what didn't Happen

I HAVE HAD A SLIGHT FEELING of nostalgia during the past few days. Indeed, my mind has been full of a little incident that occurred when I was a boy of nine. It is as vivid in my memory as though it happened only yesterday.

I was standing on top of a wall at the time on the corner of the street where I lived. With all the foolhardiness and bravado of childhood I began to run backwards and forwards along the top of the wall, getting faster and faster all the time. My mother, who had never any trouble in making her feelings known, told me in no uncertain terms to come down at once. I was slightly annoyed and rather embarrassed at being shown up in front of my friends – but experience had taught me to do what I was told. So I came down and stood in front of my mother. She was a wonderful and, in many ways, a unique character. Wagging her finger at me she said, 'Now, remember what happened to you the last time you ran so fast along the top of that wall. You fell and split your head open.' 'But, mum', I said, quite truthfully, 'that never happened to me.' With a twinkle in her eye she replied, 'Never mind, remember it anyway!'

Now there is a true piece of Irish philosophy for you – 'Remember what didn't happen'. But, like most Irish philosophy, it is not as silly as it sounds. You see, we tend only to remember the things that happen, especially the unpleasant things, like the day when the car broke down and we arrived too late to see our son receive his school prize; or the Sunday morning when we put a nail through the hot-water pipe and had to tear up the floorboards and keep our thumb over the hole till the plumber arrived; or the Saturday evening when four of our friends turned up for dinner and we'd forgotten they were coming – and the 'cupboard was bare!'; or the night when we fell asleep while driving on the M1 and only the sudden and loud blare of music from the car radio jolted us awake and saved us from disaster.

Now, of course, we don't live our lives in constant crisis. Ninety-nine per cent of our lives are uneventful. What is the point of recalling the routine, the mundane or the inconsequential? Well, just that! The hundreds of times when the car didn't break down and we kept our appointments; the scores of nails we have hammered in safely, give or take the occasional sore thumb; the dozens of friends we have been able to welcome to our home and our table without embarrassment; and the thousands of miles we've travelled on the motorways of Britain without falling asleep and without mishap, accident or injury.

I know it sounds a bit Irish. It seems an odd use of memory to remember things that didn't happen. But the providence of God is worth pondering. In multitudes of everyday situations in which God may be farthest from our minds he watches over us in love. We will complain less about the mundane and become more positive about the routine if we have the wisdom to remember, with gratitude, the things that didn't happen.

SCRIPTURES TO READ

> I lift up my eyes to the mountains;
>   where is my help to come from?
> My help comes from Yahweh
>   who made heaven and earth.
>
> May he save your foot from stumbling;
>   may he, your guardian, not fall asleep!
> You see – he neither sleeps nor slumbers,
>   the guardian of Israel.
>
> Yahweh is your guardian, your shade,
>   Yahweh, at your right hand.
> By day the sun will not strike you,
>   nor the moon by night.
>
> Yahweh guards you from all harm
>   Yahweh guards your life,
> Yahweh guards your comings and goings,
>   henceforth and for ever.
>
>   (Psalm 121)

A PRAYER TO USE

We thank you, O God, for your constant care of us, even when we are unaware of it, and for your protection in times of danger. May we never forget your goodness, always rejoice in your love and trust in your faithfulness.

13

Too Busy

I WAS LUCKY ENOUGH to see my four young grand-children the other day and played my usual trick to keep them occupied during a wet spell. Digging out a large box of old family photographs I started them on a game of 'Spot granny and grandad'. It never fails! Before long there were hoots of laughter and gasps of disbelief as they discovered ancient snaps of their grandparents, taken at a very tender age.

It sounded such good fun that I decided to have a go myself and within minutes I was on a trip down memory lane. Photographs of forgotten scenes of my children building sand-castles by the sea, or kicking a football in the garden, thrilled me. But, I must admit, there was a little bit of pain as well as I realised that I couldn't recover those years. They had passed like a flash and they were gone forever. As I looked back I began to wonder, 'Had I been too busy to enjoy my children growing up and had I done enough to develop my friend-ship with them?'

It is a question many of us have to face. In spite of

the increased leisure time available we seem to be busier and more preoccupied than ever. For instance, there are some people I hate telephoning because they always give the impression that I am interrupting them doing something far more important. And I am frequently embarrassed by a variation on a similar theme. It happens when people, introducing me as a guest speaker, go on at great length and even greater exaggeration about how busy I am and how fortunate they are to have me with them. On such occasions I don't know where to put myself and I sometimes wish the ground would open and swallow me up.

Perhaps the most embarrassing and certainly the most painful moment for me was when a woman, who had obviously needed my help, said, 'I would have asked you but you were too busy!' Now that really did touch a sore spot. I had obviously given the impression that I was too busy to care.

Of course, I don't think I am alone in this. Every day I meet people who are too busy. Some people are too busy because that's the way they like it. They function better like that. Some are too busy because they dare not stop and think – their thoughts would be too painful. Some are too busy because the nature of their job demands it and, apparently, there is no escape from it. Others are too busy because they have never learned to say 'no'. But all the time life is passing us by. Friendships are allowed to lapse, family life suffers, and that richness and fulfilment of life which our ceaseless activity is meant to achieve, is always just out of reach.

Some years ago, in the midst of my own too busy life, I had a serious heart attack. It taught me a lot of things, including the fact that God has a sense of humour, for my work went on and flourished without me. So, I have learnt some lessons. I am still busy but not too busy. I have discovered that sometimes I can get more work done by standing still than by running around like a mad thing. The most important lesson of all is that, in the midst of all the necessary and time-consuming activities of daily life, I must never be too busy to care for people – for people matter more than things.

SCRIPTURES TO READ

As tenderly as a father treats his children,
so Yahweh treats those who fear him;
he knows of what we are made,
he remembers that we are dust.

As for a human person – his days are like grass,
he blooms like the wild flowers;
as soon as the wind blows he is gone,
never to be seen there again.

But Yahweh's faithful love for those who fear him
is from eternity and for ever;
and his saving justice to their children's children;
as long as they keep his covenant,
and carefully obey his precepts.

(Psalm 103:13–18)

In the course of their journey he came to a village, and a woman named Martha welcomed him into her house. She had a sister called Mary, who sat down at the Lord's feet and listened to him speaking. Now Martha, who was distracted with all the serving, came to him and said, 'Lord, do you not care that my sister is leaving me to do the serving all by myself? Please tell her to help me.' But the Lord answered, 'Martha, Martha,' he said, 'you worry and fret about so many things, and yet few are needed, indeed only one. It is Mary who has chosen the better part, and it is not to be taken from her.'

(Luke 10:38–42)

A PRAYER TO USE

O God, Creator of time and space, help us to create space in our crowded lives that we might learn to rest in you, to grow as people and to spend time caring for those who need us most.

14

Leaving Room for Surprises

IN MY LINE OF BUSINESS, as you may imagine, I get many requests for my services. But the one I got just before midnight on a Saturday would come as a surprise to most people. The telephone rang at ten to twelve and, since that is not an uncommon occurrence, I had my dressing gown close to hand and got quickly out of bed to answer the call. As soon as I picked up the receiver a slightly inebriated female voice said, 'Can you pick me up in ten minutes outside the Mucky Duck' which, being interpreted, means outside the Black Swan.

Now it isn't always easy to see the funny side of things at that time of the night, especially if you have been wakened out of a deep sleep by a wrong number. But when I told my wife the nature of the call we couldn't get to sleep for an hour laughing about it.

Of course the explanation is fairly simple. There is a local taxi company with a telephone number almost exactly like mine – so I frequently get invited out at midnight! And I very often get orders of another kind during the day, for the entry next to mine in the telephone directory is Bishops Confectionery Limited. So on occasions I am asked to deliver, as a matter of urgency, two gross of Liquorice All Sorts, one gross of Smarties and six boxes of Quality Street. There then follows that marvellous moment when I have to reveal that they are talking to the wrong Bishop and that the only thing I can deliver is religion. Their response ranges from acute embarrassment to a lively banter, usually at my expense. Wrong numbers can be very frustrating. They can also be great fun.

The one I like best came early one evening a few months ago. When I answered the call and said who I was there was an immediate and audible gasp at the other end of the line, followed by a momentary silence. Then a voice, that I didn't recognise, said, 'Well, I didn't want to talk to a bishop but now that you're there, can I have a quick word?' Now wild horses wouldn't drag from me the detail of the ensuing conversation. But it was one in which I was able to offer pastoral care to a person in great need and, at the same time, receive help in return. That surprise encounter on the telephone enriched the lives of both of us.

There is a famous story in the Bible which is very similar. A Samaritan woman came to a well to draw out water. While she was there Jesus came and asked her for a drink. In responding to his simple request she was taken completely by surprise, for she encountered in the unknown, thirsty traveller none other than the Son of God.

In the ordinary things of life we need to leave room for surprises, to leave room for God to encounter us in unexpected people and places; in experiences, sometimes sorrowful, sometimes joyful, sometimes puzzling, in which God comes to us and says, 'Now, you weren't

will become a spring of water within, welling up
for eternal life.

(John 4:3–14)

A PRAYER TO USE

Lord, it is not always the things that happen to us, but
our reactions to them, that prove decisive and creative
in our lives. Help us, therefore, in the surprises that
come to be aware of your Spirit, to recognise your way
and to respond to your will.

15

Love Yourself

ONE OF THE WALLS in my study is covered with picture postcards that friends have sent me from all over the world. Pride of place, at the moment, has been given to one I recently received from Killarney on the south-eastern tip of Ireland. The picture on this particular card especially warmed my heart for it reminded me of the honeymoon that my wife and I spent in that lovely part of the world many years ago.

It also recalled to mind something that I would prefer to forget and have never succeeded in living down. You will find this difficult to believe, but it is absolutely true. While I was on honeymoon I preached two sermons – and I wasn't even ordained at the time.

On reflection, I must have been crackers. There are many interesting things to do while on honeymoon but I managed – through circumstances beyond my control – to allow myself to be pushed into a pulpit not once but twice! I can't for the life of me remember what I said but my wife insists I should have taken as my text the words from Luke's Gospel, 'I have married a wife and I cannot come.'

Two is company and three may be a crowd, but, if you happen to be on honeymoon, two congregations are a disaster. Still, I have survived the experience and so has my marriage. But the arrival of that picture postcard set me thinking about that familiar saying, 'Two's company, three's a crowd.' Of course we all know what it means but I don't think it's as completely true as some would have us believe.

I move across the country a lot and meet a great many people from a whole variety of backgrounds and as I have done so I have discovered a very interesting fact. There are a considerable number of people who enjoy the company of others but can't stand their own company. Now I am not talking about the fear of loneliness which most of us have to cope with from time to time. I am talking about people who simply cannot bear to be alone with their own thoughts and so they smother them, or bury them, in noise or activity or amongst crowds of other people. For them, 'Two's company, one's a crowd', for they are overwhelmed by their own company. To put it another way, though it may seem strange to do so, they don't love themselves.

Yet Jesus made it quite clear that we ought to have a proper love for ourselves. He said that we must love our neighbours as ourselves. In other words it is OK to love ourselves. Indeed if we fail to love ourselves as children of God how can we possibly learn to love other people? God knows what he is doing. He loves us. He knows both the best and the worst about us and he accepts us as we are. We must learn to love what God loves. We must learn to accept what God accepts. That doesn't mean we must stand in front of a mirror and say to our image, 'I love you more and more'. But it does mean that what God loves I must not despise.

SCRIPTURES TO READ

One of the scribes who had listened to them debating appreciated that Jesus had given a good answer and put a further question to him, 'Which is the first of all the commandments?' Jesus replied, 'This is the first: Listen, Israel, the Lord our God is the one, only Lord, and you must love the Lord your God with all your heart, with all your soul, with all your mind and with all your strength. The second is this: You must love your neighbour as yourself. There is no other commandment greater than these.' The scribe said to him, 'Well spoken, Master; what you have said is true, that he is one and there is no other. To love him with all your heart, with all your understanding and strength, and to love your neighbour as yourself, this is far more important than any burnt offering or sacrifice.' Jesus, seeing how wisely he had spoken, said, 'You are not far from the kingdom of God.'

(Mark 12:28–34)

A PRAYER TO USE

O God, you have shown your love for us in the gift of your only Son. May we not despise that love by failing to have a proper love for ourselves. Rather may we so rejoice at your goodness in creating us free and unique persons that we respond by giving you first place in our affections and by loving you with all our heart, soul, mind and strength, and our neighbour as ourselves.

16

Programmed by Prejudice

BISHOPS ARE MEANT TO BE shepherds of a human flock but last summer I had a unique experience of the real thing. I became the shepherd of a flock of real sheep, the four-legged variety.

I was paying a pastoral visit to a sheep farm and, at the same time, enjoying one of the hottest days of the year. The farmer and I had just entered a field, in which were scattered about two hundred sheep, when he suddenly turned to me and said, 'I have a surprise for you, Roy.' He pointed to the sheep, handed me his shepherd's crook and said, 'A bishop is called to be the shepherd of a flock. Well, there it is. I want you to round up those sheep and bring them into this corner of the field.'

I was flabbergasted or, as they say in that part of the world, I was 'gob-smacked'. I said to the farmer, 'Are you not going to give me some help?' 'I'll lend you my two sheep dogs,' he replied, 'and I'll teach you how to whistle.' Well, you can't ask for fairer than that, can you?

'If you give one long whistle, moving from a low note to a high note,' he said, 'the dogs will run away from you, one going left and one going right, and both will finish up behind the sheep.' So I tried it and it worked – first time! You could have knocked me down with a feather. 'Now, Jim,' I said to the farmer, 'so far so good, but how do I get them back bringing the sheep with them?' 'Reverse the whistle', he said. 'This time, one long whistle but moving from a high note to a low note.' And, blow me, it worked again. The dogs, moving left and right, brought the sheep to me. How I wish I could organise my diocese as easily as that! It gave me a tremendous feeling of satisfaction and achievement.

But the question that remained uppermost in my mind

was, 'How can the same whistle make two dogs go in opposite directions?' 'Simple,' said Jim, 'they are trained separately. One is trained to go left when that whistled instruction is given and the other is trained to go right.' I suppose, to put it another way, they were programmed.

I have been thinking a lot about that unique experience of mine and I have come to the conclusion that it has something quite important to say to us, namely, that many of the conflicts, even the minor ones, we have in this world come about because in one way or another we are all 'programmed'. Of course I don't mean that we have no freedom of action, but rather that we severely limit the freedom that is ours by allowing ourselves to become set in our ways. We become conditioned by our history, our environment, our culture, our prejudices. The same incident, or the same truth, is perceived in totally opposite ways by different people, each of whom claims that his or her interpretation is the only right one.

All I know is that both sheepdogs were needed to produce the required result. There would have been no unity in that particular flock, and no thrill and satisfaction for this particular shepherd, if opposites had not combined to produce harmony and purpose. Think about it.

SCRIPTURES TO READ

> Jesus spoke to them:
> I am the good shepherd;
> I know my own
> and my own know me,
> just as the Father knows me
> and I know the Father;

and I lay down my life for my sheep.
And there are other sheep I have
that are not of this fold,
and I must lead these too.
They too will listen to my voice,
and there will be only one flock,
one shepherd.
The Father loves me,
because I lay down my life
in order to take it up again.
No one takes it from me;
I lay it down of my own free will,
and as I have power to lay it down,
so I have power to take it up again;
and this is the command I have received from
    my Father.

These words caused a fresh division among the Jews.
Many said, 'He is possessed, he is raving; why do you
listen to him?' Others said, 'These are not the words
of a man possessed by a devil: could a devil open the
eyes of the blind?'

(John 10:14–21)

A PRAYER TO USE

Thank you, O God, for the gift of freedom you have
given to your children. May we value it deeply and use
it wisely. Keep us from becoming set in our ways or
imprisoned in our prejudices and help us so to respect
the opinions of those who differ from us that together
we might achieve understanding, purpose and harmony.

17

Love never Fails

RECENTLY I HAD ONE OF those experiences that are usually kept for nightmares. Along with five other people whom I had never met before I was stuck in a lift midway between the fourth and fifth floors of a London office block. My five companions were all friends and so, as you might imagine, their initial reaction was one of bravado and bonhomie. Banter and laughter were the order of the day – for about thirty seconds! Then we moved on to the frantic button-pushing stage accompanied by loud calls for help.

Three of my travelling companions then went all silent and one looked decidedly 'peaky'. She had turned a whiter shade of pale and it was obvious that she was beginning to suffer from claustrophobia. Of the remaining pair one was a singer and the other a joker. The singer decided to entertain us with a raucous rendition of 'Oh, why are we waiting', while the joker turned his attention to me. Spotting my dog-collar, he said, 'What have you been doing to deserve this, vicar?' 'Can't you put a word in with the gentleman upstairs?' he went on, and I don't think he was referring to the lift engineer.

Fortunately at that moment there was a humming noise followed by a sharp jolt and the lift began to move downwards. We reached the ground floor safely and, with a great sense of relief, we all tumbled out into fresh air and freedom. My travelling companions didn't give me any credit for their deliverance and, to be fair, I didn't claim any for I was just as relieved as they were when those doors opened and we escaped.

We had only been stuck for four minutes but it seemed like eternity. It wasn't pleasant to be trapped, even for such a short time, and I was delighted to be free. But the incident forced me to reflect on hundreds of people known to me, who, because life has treated them harshly, are unable to get free from the circumstances surrounding them. I thought of people like Joyce, who has sacrificed the normality of life and the prospect of marriage in order to look after infirm and ageing parents. My mind went to those like George and Ruth, whose entire life has been shaped by the need to give constant care and support to their profoundly handicapped son. And I also thought of others like James, whose social life is virtually non-existent because of the time he commits to caring for his wife Susan, who suffers from multiple sclerosis.

In a lifetime spent working closely with people, those for whom I have the highest regard and from whom I have sometimes received the greatest encouragement, are those who, though apparently trapped by circumstances, manage to triumph over them.

One of the unkind taunts directed at Jesus concerned his inability to triumph over circumstances. 'If you are who you say you are, come down from the cross', was the substance of the jeers of his enemies. But, of course, they had missed the point. It was not nails that bound him to the cross. It was love that held him there. It is love, mixed with a fair amount of courage, that enables Joyce, George and Ruth, James and Susan and a host of others like them to triumph over their circumstances. It is their courage and their patience that enable them to prove what Jesus knew to be true – that love never fails.

SCRIPTURES TO READ

Above his head was placed the charge against him; it read: 'This is Jesus, the King of the Jews.' Then two bandits were crucified with him, one on the right and one on the left.

The passers-by jeered at him; they shook their heads and said, 'So you would destroy the Temple and in three days rebuild it! Then save yourself if you are God's son and come down from the cross!' The chief priests and the scribes and elders mocked him in the same way, with the words, 'He saved others; he cannot save himself. He is the king of Israel; let him come down from the cross now, and we will believe in him. He has put his trust in God; now let God rescue him if he wants him. For he did say, "I am God's son." ' Even the bandits who were crucified with him taunted him in the same way.

(Matthew 27:37–44)

Love is always patient and kind . . . It is always ready to make allowances, to trust, to hope and to endure whatever comes. Love never comes to an end.

(1 Corinthians 13:4, 7–8)

A PRAYER TO USE

Give us grace, O Lord, to face adverse circumstances with courage and to encourage others to do the same. May the knowledge that love never fails be a source of comfort, inspiration and hope to all who suffer.

18

Wishful Thinking

ON THE MORNING OF A RECENT Test match at Headingley I came across a ten-year-old boy who was not only in the England team but was also winning the game single-handed. I was walking along the back of some gardens near my home when I heard this lad going through all the motions of playing cricket for England. With cricket stumps chalked on the garage door and a tennis ball gripped firmly in his hand he was giving a running commentary on himself bowling, fielding and batting his side to victory against the Australians. He had assumed the name of Ian Botham. It didn't matter to him that Botham wasn't playing in the Test match. As far as he was concerned he should have been playing and he was!

Imagination is a wonderful thing. One moment he was Ian Botham bowling out the Australian captain and the next he was Botham taking a brilliant slip catch. Five minutes later he was Botham hitting four sixes in one over to win the match. He didn't even notice me as I stood and watched for he was in a world of his own;

that wonderful world of make-believe that we all inhabit from time to time. It is not just a game that children play. There is a touch of Eliza Doolittle's 'Oh, wouldn't it be loverley' in all of us.

How often, in the flattering acoustics of the bathroom, have we convinced ourselves that we are singing like Pavarotti, Julie Andrews, Cliff Richard or Madonna? Come the Wimbledon tennis tournament how many of us will live out our fantasies in terms of Steffi Graf or Stefan Edberg? And, if Jim ever 'fixes' it for me, I will be the conductor of a world famous orchestra playing the Rodetsky March. To wave my baton to control such musical talent and produce such a glorious sound would be the experience of a lifetime.

It's funny when you think about it. In our world of make-believe we are nearly always 'winners', always successful, always larger than life. In all my dreams and imaginings I would never cast myself, for instance, as the player of the triangle in that great orchestra. Yet even the triangle has an important part to play. The composer of the music has written the triangle into the score and if the sound of the triangle is missing the music is incomplete.

Whoever we are and wherever we are it is vital to remember that we have a unique contribution to make to the wholeness and harmony of life and society – simply by being ourselves and not some cardboard cut-out of a make-believe character. Too many people regret that they are not someone else. What a waste. We must have confidence in being ourselves. By all means let us enjoy to the full those harmless moments of make-believe. But at the end of the day each of us needs to be convinced that '*It is OK to be me.*'

SCRIPTURES TO READ

Seeing the crowds, Jesus went onto the mountain. And when he was seated his disciples came to him. Then he began to speak. This is what he taught them:

> How blessed are the poor in spirit:
> the kingdom of Heaven is theirs.
> Blessed are the gentle:
> they shall have the earth as inheritance.
> Blessed are those who mourn:
> they shall be comforted.
> Blessed are those who hunger and thirst
>   for uprightness:
> they shall have their fill.
> Blessed are the merciful:
> they shall have mercy shown them.
> Blessed are the pure in heart:
> they shall see God.
> Blessed are the peacemakers:
> they shall be recognised as
>   children of God.
> Blessed are those who are persecuted
>   in the cause of uprightness:
> the kingdom of Heaven is theirs.

(Matthew 5:1–10)

The Son of God . . . loved me and gave himself for me.

(Galatians 2:20)

A PRAYER TO USE

God of all creation, we thank you for the gifts and skills you have given to each one of us. Enable us to admire the talents of others without envy, to recognise our own without false modesty and to use them with confidence for the benefit of all.

19

God is on Our Side

ONE OF THE RISKS of being a bishop is that I get 'wheeled out' onto platforms to speak on a whole variety of occasions. Apparently the fallacy exists that bishops can speak on any subject imaginable and on every occasion possible. The temptation is to believe the fallacy. I don't – and so I usually have to be dragged, kicking and screaming, onto some platforms. But I didn't hesitate when I was invited by the local Community Response organisation to say a few words on their behalf. They are a local education and training consortium whose task is to help those who, through no fault of their own, have been educationally disadvantaged.

I was asked to present award certificates and to say a few appropriate words of encouragement. It proved to be a pleasure rather than a duty and I was the one who received the greatest encouragement. I presented over one hundred certificates to a marvellous cross-section of people: men and women, young and old, married and single, black and white, Muslim and Church of England. A wonderful group of people who, for one reason or another, had been 'left behind'. They had been unable to obtain the necessary academic qualifications at school or had missed out on the skills that are essential to find employment. I gave out certificates of proficiency in office practice, needlework, catering, carpentry, art, design, computing and a host of other basic skills.

Encouraged by this initial achievement some of the students would go on to even greater challenges and succeed in nationally recognised examinations, and others, for the first time, would be given a job. But for all who received an award that night it was a unique milestone. At last they had achieved something. They were not failures. Their worth had been recognised. They had something of value to contribute to the life of their community. Their increased self-esteem and their pleasure in each other's achievement was a joy to see. Indeed it was so tangible I could almost reach out and touch it.

On reflection I think the reason why I identified so closely and so happily with this group was my own past experience of feeling 'left behind'. I didn't obtain one piece of paper to say I had achieved anything – until I was twenty-seven years old. And that only happened because a friend took me to one side, convinced me that I might have something to offer, and encouraged me to develop my potential. In other words he was sufficiently interested in me to want to bring out the best in me.

I don't think there is a nobler task than to try to bring out the best in other people. Sometimes God is portrayed as a big brother wanting to discover the worst about us so that he can punish us. Nothing could be further from the truth. Indeed, if my understanding is correct, the opposite is true. He wants to bring out the best in us

71

and help us to reach our full potential for after all it was he who put that potential there in the first place.

When I asked those students from Community Response what had encouraged them most their reply was very interesting. 'We felt that the teachers were on our side!' Perhaps that is the truest and most encouraging thing I can say to you. God is not against us. He is on our side.

SCRIPTURES TO READ

If God is for us, who can be against us? Since he did not spare his own Son, but gave him up for the sake of all of us, then can we not expect that with him he will freely give us all his gifts? Who can bring any accusation against those that God has chosen? When God grants saving justice who can condemn? Are we not sure that it is Christ Jesus, who died – yes and more, who was raised from the dead and is at God's right hand – and who is adding his plea for us? Can anything cut us off from the love of Christ – can hardships or distress, or persecution, or lack of food and clothing, or threats or violence; as scripture says:

For your sake we are being massacred all day long, treated as sheep to be slaughtered?

No; we come through all these things triumphantly victorious, by the power of him who loved us. For I am certain of this: neither death nor life, nor angels, nor principalities, nothing already in existence and nothing still to come, nor any power, nor the heights nor the depths, nor any created thing whatever, will

72

be able to come between us and the love of God,
known to us in Christ Jesus our Lord.

(Romans 8:31–9)

A PRAYER TO USE

Thank you, O God, that you are on our side and that
nothing can separate us from your love. Strengthened
by your Spirit may we follow your example in seeking
to bring out the best in other people.

20

Nothing Hidden

ONE OF MY MOST MEMORABLE and unexpected experiences came about with the help of the Central Division of the City Police Force – and it happened in the wee small hours one Saturday morning. I had asked the Chief Superintendent if I might accompany some of his officers on their period of night duty in the city. It seemed to me that if I was to understand and serve my local community, and if I was to support and encourage the local police in their vital work within that community, I ought to know what problems and pressures they encountered while most of us were asleep.

So at nine o'clock on Friday evening I turned up at Police Headquarters and stayed with the officers of the Central Division till two o'clock on Saturday morning. Now I hasten to say that no special crimes were laid on for my benefit. I had to take pot luck, but it was certainly an interesting and varied menu. I travelled at speed in a pursuing squad car and walked the streets with a constable on the beat. I joined a group of officers on visits to pubs, wine bars and night clubs and witnessed two people being arrested for street violence. Through-out the whole evening I kept a low profile, of course, never getting in the way, and leaving my dog-collar and cassock at home!

But the highlight of the experience came at two a.m. – and it was totally unexpected. After nearly five hours on the streets the Chief Superintendent took pity on me and offered to take me home in the squad car. I gladly accepted and, in the company of two officers, I was escorted home. Now the previous day, on the advice of the police following several attempted break-ins at my home, I had had security lights fitted. They were pro-grammed to come on automatically when anyone came within ten yards of the house. As yet I hadn't had a chance to try them out so I asked the driver of the squad car to stop thirty yards from my front gate. I would walk down the drive and put the efficiency of the security lights to the test.

The officer obliged and I was just saying my 'thanks and goodnights' when he interrupted me and said, 'Sir, were you expecting a caller at this hour of the morning?' 'Certainly not,' I replied. 'Well, sir, someone has just disappeared into your driveway and, if you don't mind, we'll go and have a look.' So the car moved slowly and quietly through my front gate and into the driveway – by which time the security lights were blazing and my two dogs were barking. Like a flash, the two officers jumped from the car, encircled the house in a pincer movement and reappeared holding one very surprised intruder!

Poor man. How unlucky can you get? Any self-respect-ing bishop should have been in bed at two o'clock in the morning instead of roaming the streets in a police squad car. Is there nothing sacred?!

Well, the 'good book' says, 'Be sure your sins will find you out', though most of us, if we are honest, hope for a little credit before we have to pay up. But just in case we are tempted to point the finger only at others the Bible also says, 'There is nothing hidden that will not come to the light.' Now that should make us all *pause for thought*!

SCRIPTURES TO READ

> Where shall I go to escape your spirit?
> Where shall I flee from your presence?
> If I scale the heavens you are there,
> if I lie flat in Sheol, there you are.
>
> If I speed away on the wings of the dawn,
> if I dwell beyond the ocean,
> even there your hand will be guiding me,
> your right hand holding me fast.
>
> I will say, 'Let the darkness cover me,
> and the night wrap itself around me,'
> even darkness to you is not dark,
> and night is as clear as the day.
>
> (Psalm 139:7–12)

The people had gathered in their thousands . . . and he [Jesus] began to speak, first of all to his disciples. 'Be on your guard against the yeast of the Pharisees – their hypocrisy. Everything now covered up will be uncovered, and everything now hidden will be made clear. For this reason, whatever you have said in the dark will be heard in the daylight, and what you have

whispered in hidden places will be proclaimed from
the housetops.'

(Luke 12:1–3)

A PRAYER TO USE

Thank you, O God, for all those who maintain law and
order and for those who try to help and restore those
who have been convicted of crime. Keep us free from
hypocrisy and ever aware that we are living our lives in
your sight.

21

Family Bulletins

I WONDER IF MANY OTHER PEOPLE share my experience of being on the receiving end of what have become known as Family Bulletins. My post-bag tends to get cluttered with them around Christmas but I also get a fair smattering of them throughout the year. I rarely get time to read them and usually put them to one side for a rainy day – in the hope that the weather might keep fine for months. For, to be honest, I frequently get bored to tears reading them.

Now I know that I am bound to lose a few friends over this but, as a bishop, I am also bound to tell the truth and I really do find them a trial. The same information is duplicated or photocopied by the writers and sent round all their friends. If you are lucky you may get a few handwritten words at the end. Often the Bulletins go into great and sometimes lurid detail about the progress of the children, with blow by blow accounts of life from the nappy stage right through to university entrance and beyond. The most common feature of those I receive is that all of the writer's children are doing much better than mine. Their intellectual ability is astounding and their musical talents are outstanding. Fifty per cent of them seem to be doing their grade eight flute and the other fifty per cent their grade eight piano. Oh dear! I was looking forward to going to heaven – but not if it is full of flautists and pianists, all with grade eight certificates!

Seriously though, it is always a joy to hear from old friends and to discover how life has been treating them. Memory is such a beautiful thing and to have it refreshed

and renewed is very enriching. But I have discovered something quite significant regarding one particular aspect of my life as a bishop. I write dozens of letters each day. Of necessity they have to be type-written or word-processed. But my friends tell me that those letters which are in my own handwriting, however difficult they may be to read, are always welcomed more and treasured longer. Maybe that is because I keep them fairly brief but it is also, I believe, because the handwritten word may convey a greater sense of personal communication between friends.

One of the greatest gifts that we can possess is that of communicating to other people that we value them for what they are. At times we are all prone to cultivate the friendship of others because of the use they can be to us – but to affirm people for what they are is a rare and wonderful gift. Jesus had it. When he was in conversation with a man, woman or child he gave them his undivided attention. He wasn't looking round the room for someone more important to talk to. He saw infinite value in the person before him. There was no more important person than the one to whom he was speaking at that moment. The whole pattern of his life and work, indeed the whole cast of his mind, emphasised the value he placed on the individual.

I believe that this gift of valuing others is specially communicated by direct speech or practical loving action. But where distance makes this impossible, then a caring, handwritten letter can be a source of great affirmation and personal friendship. Is there a friend of ours today for whom a handwritten letter from us would be a source of real encouragement? Why not pick up the pen? It is not only mightier than the sword – it is usually more powerful than the word-processor!

SCRIPTURES TO READ

Make your own the mind of Christ Jesus:

Who, being in the form of God,
did not count equality with God
something to be grasped.

But he emptied himself,
taking the form of a slave,
becoming as human beings are;
and being in every way like a human being,
he was humbler yet,
even to accepting death, death on a cross.

And for this God raised him high,
and gave him the name
which is above all other names;

so that all beings
in the heavens, on earth and in the underworld,
should bend the knee at the name of Jesus
and that every tongue should acknowledge
Jesus Christ as Lord,
to the glory of God the Father.

(Philippians 2:5–11)

A PRAYER TO USE

Thank you, O Lord, for the value you have placed on us by sharing our humanity even to the point of death. Help us so to make your mind our own that all we say and do may serve to affirm and encourage all that is good in others.

22

Strength in Weakness

WALKING BRISKLY FOR FOUR or five miles is one of my more enjoyable daily occupations. It enables me to think; gets me away from the telephone and, above all, helps to keep me fit. My puny effort at keeping fit, though, is put in the shade by the scores of joggers that I meet, pounding the pavements, especially at weekends. They seem to come in all shapes and sizes, all ages and conditions. Some are in such superb physical condition that I envy them. Others appear to be in such obvious distress that I find myself praying that they will get home safely!

But I must say, I am impressed by their discipline, their determination to keep going and their dedication to the cause of fitness. In many ways they reflect a predominant characteristic of today's culture. There is a premium on physical fitness, strength and competitiveness and there's no harm in that, for we all love a winner.

However, I had a rather unique experience with a group of people who, in normal circumstances, would be considered losers. I had responded to an invitation to visit a local school where the twenty-one pupils, aged from five to sixteen, were profoundly handicapped – both physically and mentally impaired. Fitness, strength and competitiveness were not on the agenda. Indeed sometimes progress was measured by the movement of a finger or the recognition of a colour, or by a gentle smile of appreciation and gratitude.

Here was weakness personified and yet it had a strength to move me as I have rarely been moved before. I was moved by the patience and love of parents; by the skill and dedication of teachers and, most of all, by the handicapped children and young people themselves. Their vulnerability was massive. Their hold on life was very fragile and yet they communicated something very powerful to me. All my natural feelings of helplessness, despair and even anger which began to come to the surface were, in a quite remarkable way, pushed to one side. It seemed to me that a light was shining from these children and young people that caused a well of love to spring up within me.

In order to speak to some of them or look into the eyes of others I had to kneel beside them. There was something symbolic about that – because I found myself on the receiving end of a blessing. Indeed, being back at school again, I found myself being taught a simple yet profound lesson, namely, not to walk away from people in pain, disability or handicap, but to walk towards them and touch them. Hope and love can spring from the wounds of brokenness.

I suppose this is one of the reasons why Jesus spent so much time with the so-called losers of his society, and why the cross – that most powerful sign of the faith – is also a symbol of vulnerability and weakness. I am sure it also explains why, as I thought about these things, I recalled the words of the old Persian proverb:

> Don't walk in front of me, I might not follow you
> Don't walk behind me, I cannot see you
> Walk by my side – and be my friend.

SCRIPTURES TO READ

So they came to the house of the president of the synagogue, and Jesus noticed all the commotion, with people weeping and wailing unrestrainedly. He went in and said to them, 'Why all this commotion and crying? The child is not dead, but asleep.' But they ridiculed him. So he turned them all out and, taking with him the child's father and mother and his own companions, he went into the place where the child lay. And taking the child by the hand he said to her, '*Talitha kum!*' which means, 'Little girl, I tell you to get up.' The little girl got up at once and began to walk about, for she was twelve years old.

(Mark 5:38–42)

I was given a thorn in the flesh . . . I have three times pleaded with the Lord that it might leave me; but he has answered me, 'My grace is enough for you: for power is at full stretch in weakness.' . . . It is when I am weak that I am strong.

(2 Corinthians 12:7–10)

A PRAYER TO USE

Give your strength, O Lord, to those who are most vulnerable in our society, and grant your special grace to their families and friends. In a world that glorifies power, help us never to despise weakness and to remember that real strength lies in quietness, trust and integrity.

23

Green Wellies

For a bishop to be seen wearing a purple cassock would cause few people to raise an eyebrow. After all, it is part of my so-called uniform, a kind of episcopal undergarment. But when it was worn with a pair of green wellies then it did bring a smile to the lips of the congregation. Of course, they didn't do very much for the cause of colour coordination but they did keep me from sinking without trace in a sea of mud. I was walking at the time across a rain-lashed, wind-swept piece of ground on which, until very recently, had stood a magnificent church building.

Just a few weeks before, the Sunday morning congregation at St Margaret's had said their prayers unaware of two things: the first was that huge cracks were beginning to appear in the stone arches above their heads; the second was that they would never again worship in that lovely church building. Apparently their church, some seventy-eight years ago, had been built on a seam of clay. The clay had become waterlogged, the foundations had moved and the building was in imminent danger of collapse. The experts had declared that there was no real economic alternative to demolition.

As you can imagine the members of the congregation were shattered. It was their spiritual home. Much of their lives and many of their significant memories were bound up with that building. The great pivotal points of human existence, birth, marriage and death, had all been celebrated in that place. One Sunday they were worshipping in it, and the next – the doors were closed. It was considered too dangerous even to hold a farewell service in it.

But one Sunday afternoon that was put to rights – hence my green wellies! The building had been demolished. With the help of bulldozers the rubble had been cleared, the site levelled and now, towering ten foot high out of the sea of mud, stood a large wooden cross made from the roof-timbers of the old building. Beneath it stood the congregation of St Margaret's. Their church building was gone but their faith was still intact. Out of the ashes of disaster new life was beginning to rise.

Now in church terms such a story, though absolutely true, is a rare occurrence. But every day in life there are people who face disaster of similar proportions. Their business collapses or their health fails or their partner dies and their life lies in ruins – demolished by circumstances beyond their control. And no amount of clever words or pious platitudes can bring comfort to those in such dire trouble. Over the years, when trying to help people overtaken by such disasters, I have learned to stop talking and instead to point to the cross – the symbol of hope even in the darkest hour.

At the core of the Christian faith stands a Friday called Good; though it was a day of disaster, when evil, darkness and death seemed to get the upper hand. But no! As Martin Luther King said, 'Goodness defeated is stronger than evil triumphant.' The cross, like that one emerging from the sea of mud on the site of the old church, has become a symbol of hope because it leads to resurrection. With God, disaster never has the last word.

SCRIPTURES TO READ

They then took charge of Jesus, and carrying his own cross he went out to the Place of the Skull or, as it is called in Hebrew, Golgotha, where they crucified him with two others, one on either side, Jesus being in the middle. Pilate wrote out a notice and had it fixed to the cross; it ran 'Jesus the Nazarene, King of the Jews'.

(John 19:17–19)

In the evening of that same day, the first day of the week, the doors were closed in the room where the disciples were, for fear of the Jews. Jesus came and stood among them. He said to them, 'Peace be with you,' and, after saying this, he showed them his hands and his side. The disciples were filled with joy at seeing the Lord, and he said to them again, 'Peace be with you.'

(John 20:19–21)

Blessed be God the Father of our Lord Jesus Christ, who in his great mercy has given us a new birth into a living hope through the resurrection of Jesus Christ from the dead and into a heritage that can never be spoilt or soiled and never fade away.

(1 Peter 1:3–4)

A PRAYER TO USE

Lord, when unexpected tragedy comes and you seem distant from us, help us to remember that you are the God of the resurrection, and hold us in your love until our hope is rekindled and we experience your peace.

24

Silent Sermons

Y OU MAY BE SURPRISED TO LEARN that I very rarely have to listen to sermons. Some people would say that that is one of the reasons why I manage to keep so cheerful. But though I don't often hear sermons I very frequently see them and I have seen three super ones in the past few weeks. On each occasion the preacher was a woman.

The first one was playing the church organ. Nothing very strange about that, you might say, until you discovered that she was well over one hundred years old. Incredible. She had been playing that organ for longer than anyone in the congregation could remember. If I was that age I would consider it a major achievement to find the organ. But to play it as well – now that is wonderful.

The second sermon I saw involved a comparatively young woman – only seventy-nine years old! She had suffered a severe stroke and was housebound. When I called to see her I felt anxious and apologetic about bringing her to the door to let me in and quite embarrassed when she insisted on walking me to the garden gate afterwards. 'Oh, don't worry', she said, 'it's no trouble. Besides, I'm in training.' And she was. She was so determined to get better, and at the same time to support a local charity, that she had got most of the village to sponsor her to do a three hundred yard walk to the Post Office to collect her pension. I must confess to feeling a twinge of conscience as I left her and travelled home by car.

The third sermon was perhaps the most remarkable of all. The preacher wasn't aware that I was listening to her unspoken sermon – because she was blind. Her silent message was being preached in the crowded Out Patients' Department of a large city hospital. I was there purely on a pastoral visit but, surrounded by so many anxious people, I was beginning to feel a little vulnerable myself.

It was then I saw the woman concerned carrying a white stick and moving slowly but purposefully down the long hospital corridor. She hadn't brought her own affliction to be dealt with. Instead she was pushing her sick husband in a wheelchair towards the room where he would be seen by the doctor. Nursing assistants were around to help if necessary but it was obvious that this was something she wished to do by herself, as far as possible. It was an amazing sight and I shall never forget it – which is more than I can say of most of the sermons I have heard.

The common feature in all three visible sermons was a personal courage that was strong enough to overcome adverse circumstances in order to serve other people. On reflection I have to say that the things that inspire me most in daily life are the unsung and often unseen displays of courage in the lives of ordinary people. People who pick up the pieces of their broken lives and put them together again in order to contribute something of infinite value to their community and to their friends. The German proverb got it absolutely right when it declared, 'Great things are done more through courage than through wisdom.' I believe that is why God placed such importance on courage – because it was something which ordinary people could achieve. 'Be strong and of good courage', he said. 'Don't be frightened and don't be discouraged, for the Lord your God will be with you wherever you go.'

SCRIPTURES TO READ

After the death of Moses . . . the Lord said to Joshua, Moses' assistant: 'As I was with Moses, so I will be with you; I will never leave you nor forsake you. Be strong and courageous, because you will lead these people to inherit the land that I swore to their forefathers to give them. Be strong and very courageous. Be careful to obey all the law my servant Moses gave you; do not turn from it to the right or to the left, that you may be successful wherever you go. Do not let this Book of the Law depart from your mouth; meditate on it day and night, so that you may be careful to do everything written in it. Then you will be prosperous and successful. Have I not commanded you? Be strong and courageous. Do not be terrified; do not be discouraged, for the Lord your God will be with you wherever you go.'

(Joshua 1:1, 5–9 NIV)

When they saw the courage of Peter and John and realised that they were unschooled, ordinary men,

they were astonished and they took note that these
men had been with Jesus.

(Acts 4:13 NIV)

A PRAYER TO USE

Open our eyes, O Lord, to the signs of encouragement
all around us in the lives of ordinary people. We thank
you for those whose courage and fortitude inspire us and
we pray for strength to stand firm in our own times of
adversity.

25

Stereotyping

THERE WAS THIS ENGLISHMAN, this Scotsman and this Irishman. How many stories have we heard, or told, beginning with that particular formula? It is called stereotyping and it usually ends with a punch-line which reveals the Irishman as somewhat 'thicker' than the other two. I mean, only in Ireland could a person enter a Baker's shop and say, 'Is that today's bread, because yesterday's wasn't?', and receive the immediate and quite serious response, 'If you want today's bread, you will have to come back tomorrow.' As an Irishman I can perfectly understand that conversation. As far as I am concerned it makes sense – but that might reveal that there is some truth in the stereotyping!

But it is this whole question of stereotyping that worries me just a little. Our society is riddled with it. Jews are stereotyped as money-grabbing and the Scots as mean; politicians are seen as those who approach every problem with an open mouth, while bishops are those who nail their colours firmly to the fence. The media is stereotyped as selective, and therefore untrustworthy, while mothers-in-law are cruelly and unfairly portrayed as interfering busy-bodies.

But there is another and more serious, perhaps sinister form of stereotyping that is taking place. It concerns those of Asian, African or Caribbean origin. In the most unthinking manner we can classify such people as careless drivers, noisy neighbours or less intelligent than us – whoever 'us' may be. Some would consider such an attitude as both natural and acceptable in a multi-racial society. But when a whole ethnic community is branded with the folly of a few extremists it is both unfair and unwise. To stereotype all Muslims as militant, for instance, is neither helpful nor true. It is rather like saying that all Chinese look alike!

To see ourselves as others see us can be highly amusing at times, especially if we have the ability to laugh at ourselves and the exaggerated traits of our national character; like the English who go on holiday to the most exotic places and order fish and chips for tea! For myself, I find no difficulty in laughing at the multitude of Irish jokes that come my way – though my patience wears a bit thin when I'm hearing them for the umpteenth time! But stereotyping is not always fun. It can be downright dangerous when it crosses over the narrow divide into the realm of prejudice. It is when we project our prejudices and presuppositions onto other people that fear replaces fun, intolerance replaces moderation and the vital process of community building is undermined.

Our Lord was the subject of both stereotyping and prejudice. Indeed it is arguable that he died because he refused to be imprisoned within the stereotype that society had cast for him. His words and his works clearly marked him out as someone special but his enemies were blinded by the fact that he was the son of a carpenter –

and therefore a person of no real consequence. He refused to endorse the prejudices of his society. Instead, he greatly valued the poor, raised the profile of women and mixed unashamedly with social outcasts. No one was to be taken for granted. No one was insignificant. All had a unique place and part to play in the community. In the multi-racial society of our day the only future we have is a future together in mutual understanding and tolerance, in mutual trust and respect.

SCRIPTURES TO READ

Another time he [Jesus] went into the synagogue, and there was a man present whose hand was withered. And they were watching him to see if he would cure him on the Sabbath day, hoping for something to charge him with. He said to the man with the withered hand, 'Get up and stand in the middle!' Then he said to them, 'Is it permitted on the Sabbath day to do good, or to do evil; to save life, or to kill?' But they said nothing. Then he looked angrily round at them, grieved to find them so obstinate, and said to the man, 'Stretch out your hand.' He stretched it out and his hand was restored. The Pharisees went out and began at once to plot with the Herodians against him, discussing how to destroy him.

(Mark 3:1–6)

The tax collectors and sinners, however, were all crowding round to listen to him, and the Pharisees and scribes complained saying, 'This man welcomes sinners and eats with them.'

(Luke 15:1–3)

A PRAYER TO USE

Give us courage, O Lord, to stand out against actions and attitudes based on prejudice. May we have the discernment to see people as they truly are, the wisdom to speak words that heal rather than hurt and the vision to work for the harmony and wholeness of our community.